Contents

Any words appearing in the text in bold, **like this**, are explained in the glossary. You can also look out for them in 'Body language' at the bottom of each page.

Always on guard!

Have you and your body ever had "one of those days"?
In the morning you wake up and get out of bed – and stub your toe on the door post. Later in the morning you scratch your finger on a sharp edge and it bleeds a little.

In the afternoon, the chain comes off your bike, and your hands get covered with greasy dirt that you can't quite wash away. In the evening you start to feel slightly hot with a tickly nose, as if you've caught some germs and a cold is coming.

Feeling OK again

And yet, a couple of days later, you're fine! Your bruised toe and scratched skin heal, your hands are clean again, and the cold never came. Your body has coped with the problems, mended the damage and defended itself against germs.

Self defence

The human body protects itself all the time. There are always germs around, tiny and unseen. Dust and dirt are everywhere too. The body regularly rubs, bumps and knocks itself in small ways, and occasionally suffers a bigger bruise, graze or cut. But most of the time, the body deals with the problems. It has many kinds of self-defences to keep out germs, kill them if they get in, combat disease, and repair injuries and damage. As you eat, walk, talk with friends, do lessons at school, watch television, even when you are asleep – your body is always on guard.

"For the first day I felt like death warmed up. Three days later I'd never felt better."

Chloe, 14, had food poisoning but rapidly recovered.

Body Talk

Defend Yourself

er

ree

www.raintreepublishers.co.uk

Visit our website to find out more information about **Raintree** books.

To order:
☎ Phone 44 (0) 1865 888113
▤ Send a fax to 44 (0) 1865 314091
💻 Visit the Raintree bookshop at **www.raintreepublishers.co.uk**
to browse our catalogue and order online.

First published in Great Britain by Raintree,
Halley Court, Jordan Hill, Oxford, OX2 8EJ, part
of Harcourt Education.
Raintree is a registered trademark of Harcourt
Education Ltd.

Editorial: Melanie Waldron, Rosie Gordon,
and Megan Cotugno
Design: Philippa Jenkins, Lucy Owen,
and John Walker
Illustrations: Darren Linguard and Jeff Edwards
Picture Research: Mica Brancic
and Ginny Stroud-Lewis
Production: Chloe Bloom

Originated by Dot Gradations Ltd, UK
Printed and bound in China by South China
Printing Company

10 digit ISBN: 1 406 20006 2 (hardback)
13 digit ISBN: 978 1 406 20006 9
10 09 08 07 06
10 9 8 7 6 5 4 3 2 1

10 digit ISBN 1 406 20073 5 (paperback)
13 digit ISBN 978 1 406 20073 7
11 10 09 08 07
10 9 8 7 6 5 4 3 2 1

**British Library Cataloguing in
Publication Data**
Parker, Steve
Defend yourself! : the immune system. - (Body
talk)
1.Immune system - Juvenile literature
I.Title
616'.079
The immune system

A full catalogue record for this book is available
from the British Library.

Acknowledgements
The publishers would like to thank the following
for permission to reproduce photographs:
Alamy Images **pp. 36-37** (AGStockUSA,
Inc./David Reede), **pp. 26-27** (Sally and Richard
Greenhill), p. 9 (Shout); Corbis **pp. 8, 14, 17,
19, 21, 24-25, 40, 42; 40-41** (Al Fuchs/
NewSport), **pp. 20-21** (Bettmann), **p. 33**
(Cameron), **p. 13** (Layne Kennedy), **p. 7** (Sygma/
Kent Tony); Creatas **pp. 10-11**; Getty Images **p.
20** (Brand X Pictures), **pp. 38-39** (PhotoDisc), **pp.
42-p. 43** (Stone), **p. 35** (Stone/Alan Thornton);
Harcourt Education Ltd/Tudor Photography **p.
29**; PhotoDisc/ PhotoLink **pp. 4-5**; Science Photo
Library **p. 37** (AJ Photo), **p. 36** (Andrew Syred),
pp. 14-15 (Astrid & Hanns-Freider Michler), **p.
16** (BSIP VEM), **p. 38** (Edwige), **pp. 34-35** (BSIP,
Laurent), **p. 30** (Custom Medical Stock Photo),
pp. 32-33 (David Goodsell), **pp. 6-7** (David
Scharf), **pp. 12, 22** (Dr P. Marazzi), **pp. 30-31** (Dr.
John Brackenbury), **p. 24**, (Ed Reschke Peter
Arnold, Inc.), **pp. 12-13, 22-23** (Eye of Science),
pp. 8-9 (J C Revy), **p. 18** (J. L. Carson, Custom
Medical Stock, Photo), **pp. 18-19** (Lauren Shear),
pp. 16-17 (Prof. P. Motta/ Dept. Of Anatomy/
University "La Sapeinza", Rome), **p. 25** (R.
Umesh Chandran, TDR, WHO), **p. 31** (Simon
Fraser/ Dep't Of Haematology, RVI, Newcastle),
pp. 28-29 (St Bartholomew's Hospital), **p. 15**
(Steve Gschmeissner).

Cover photograph of people in protective
clothing reproduced with permission of Getty
Images/Stone/Stuart McClymont.

The author and publisher would like to thank
Ann Fullick for her assistance in the preparation
of this book.

Dedicated to the memory of Lucy Owen

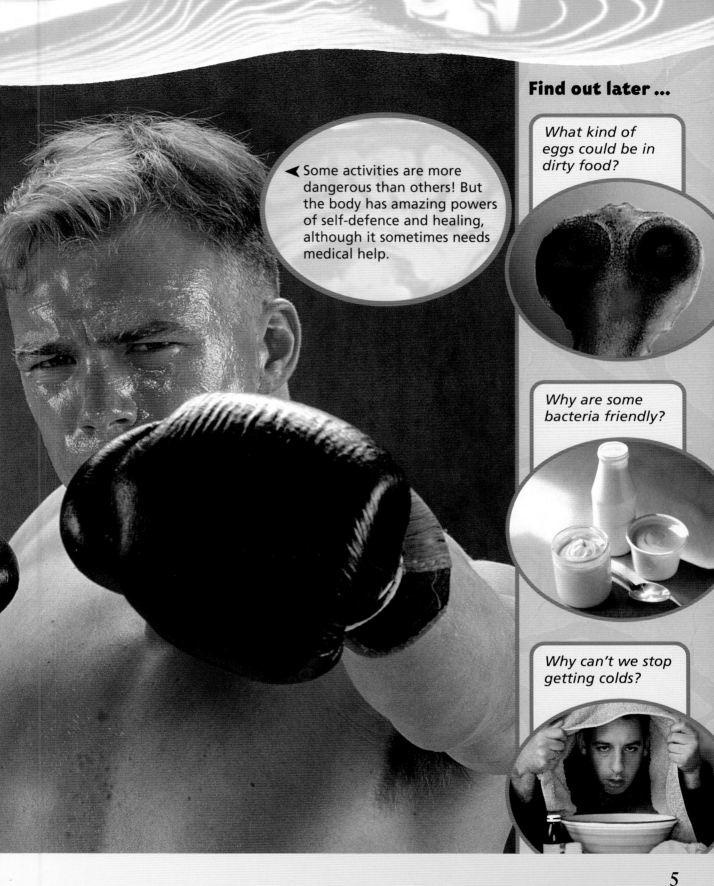

◄ Some activities are more dangerous than others! But the body has amazing powers of self-defence and healing, although it sometimes needs medical help.

Find out later ...

What kind of eggs could be in dirty food?

Why are some bacteria friendly?

Why can't we stop getting colds?

First line of defence

When people like firefighters or cold-store workers go into dangerous places, they wear protective clothing. But in a way, all our bodies have "protective clothing". It covers us almost all over, resists many kinds of harm, and even repairs itself. Of course it cannot repel serious dangers like flames or severe cold. But for day-to-day use it does a good job. This "protective clothing" is our skin.

Tough covering

Your skin has two layers, each helping to defend you. The layer you can see on the outside is the **epidermis**. It is thin but tough, stretchy yet strong. What's more, germs or scrapes cannot kill it, because it is already dead!

Even better protection

Skin makes natural oils and waxes, called **sebum**. These coat its surface and keep it bendy and stretchy. Sebum is also part of the body's defences. It keeps out water and contains natural substances that help to damage or kill germs.

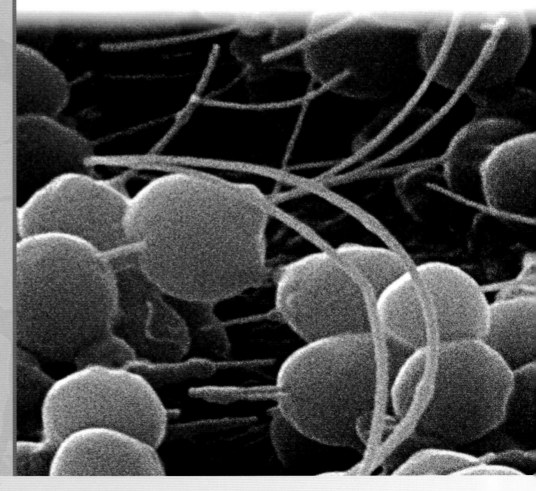

cells   microscopic "building blocks" that make up all body parts
epidermis   outer layer of skin, constantly renewed from underneath

Replace

Like all body parts, the epidermis is made of micro-sized "building blocks" called **cells**. Your whole body is made of billions and billions of cells. Most of them are very much alive and busy. But the cells of your skin's outer layer are hard, tough and dead, because they are soon worn away. They lock together like tiles on a roof or bricks in a wall, to keep out dirt, germs and other harm. As they are rubbed off, they are replaced by more dead cells, millions every hour.

Hairy cover

Tiny hairs cover most of the body, giving added defence to skin. Longer, thicker hairs on the head also protect us from a knock or the sun's fierce rays. However, the length of these hairs is up to us, depending on our haircuts and lifestyles.

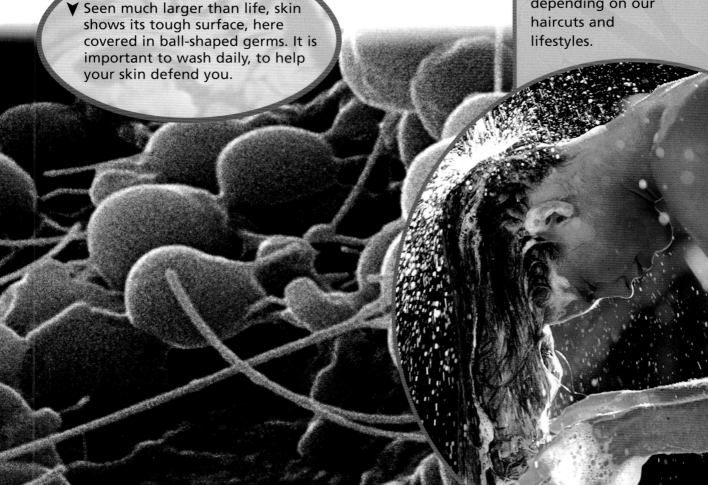

▼ Seen much larger than life, skin shows its tough surface, here covered in ball-shaped germs. It is important to wash daily, to help your skin defend you.

sebum   oily substance made by skin to protect itself and stay flexible

New "coat" every month

Every four weeks, you look like a new person! The outer layer of skin you had last month is not the same as the layer today. Tiny bits of skin gradually flake and fall off your body all the time, as you move about, wear clothes, wash and bath or shower, and rub dry afterwards. As they leave they carry with them dirt, germs and other harmful bits. This is part of the body's defences.

New for old

If skin is always flaking away from the body, why don't we end up red and raw? Because the rubbed-off bits are always being replaced by new skin from underneath. At the base of the **epidermis, cells** divide fast, to make more cells. These new cells gradually move up to the surface.

Thick-skinned!

Skin is thickest on the soles of the feet, where it gets pressed and rubbed most. Any area of skin that gets regular use responds by growing thicker, for good protection. Thickened patches of skin are called **calluses**.

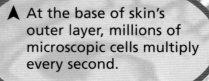

▲ At the base of skin's outer layer, millions of microscopic cells multiply every second.

calluses   patches of thick, hardened skin
keratin   tough, protein-type substance that makes skin resistant to wear

They are pushed by yet more cells below. At first they are shaped like burger buns, but after a couple of weeks they are more like pizzas. As they are forced up farther, they flatten out even more and become bent, like warped food trays.

Non-stop replacement

The whole journey for these skin cells may be just a millimetre or two. All the way through, they fill with the tough body substance called **keratin**. By the time they reach the surface, they are flat, dead and ready to be worn away.

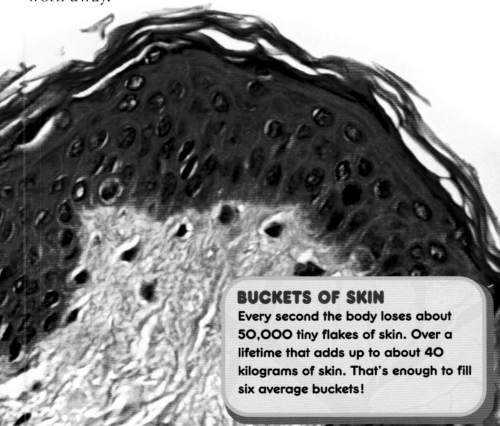

Extra help

Sometimes skin gets more than its usual wear very quickly. This can happen in just a few minutes. Then it cannot cope and may get rubbed through or swell up as blisters. Extra defences like gloves (above) stop this happening.

BUCKETS OF SKIN
Every second the body loses about 50,000 tiny flakes of skin. Over a lifetime that adds up to about 40 kilograms of skin. That's enough to fill six average buckets!

Where we feel touch

Our sense of touch comes from the lower layer of skin, the **dermis**. This has millions of tiny sensors to detect light touch, heavy pressure, heat, cold, movement and pain.

Get away!

When a pesky fly lands on your skin, you brush it away or swat it. And when danger is near, like cars on the road or the flames of a fire, you are alert and ready to move. These are more ways in which your body defends itself. Not by your body's physical structure and what it "is", but more by what it "does" – that is, what you do – your actions and movements.

Touch and feel

Your sense of touch is especially important for this kind of protection. If you detect something unusual on your skin, you want to find out what it is and whether it is harmful.

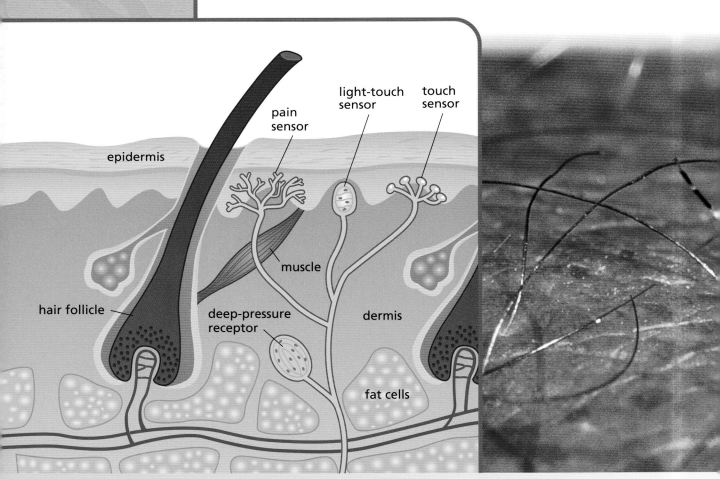

epidermis

pain sensor

light-touch sensor

touch sensor

muscle

hair follicle

deep-pressure receptor

dermis

fat cells

dermis   inner layer of skin containing sweat glands, hair roots and nerve sensors

Your sense of touch can often tell if it is hard or soft, sharp or blunt, hot or cold, rough or smooth. This helps you to judge whether all is well, or whether you need to defend yourself by taking action and perhaps moving away.

Damage limitation

If your skin does suffer harm, like a cut, bite or sting, then it warns you by feeling painful. Then your behaviour continues to protect your body. You act to limit the damage. You wash and clean the area, and maybe put on a sticking plaster. You are extra-careful not to press or knock the area, so that it heals fast. In this way your actions and behaviour help your body to defend itself.

Automatic defence

Sometimes our brains are too busy to notice a sudden danger. So the body has its own built-in defence actions, called **reflexes**. They are fast and automatic, happening before we even realize, like pulling the hand away if it touches a hot plate.

▼ Mosquitos and other pests spread germs. Our skin usually detects when they land, so we can brush them off and protect ourselves.

"RUB IT BETTER"

After a sudden knock, it helps to rub the part. This makes the skin send lots of touch messages to the brain. For a time, these "block out" some of the pain messages, so the pain isn't quite so bad.

Just a scratch ...

Where did you last cut or scratch yourself? Did it bleed much? One of your body's best defenders is your blood. Usually it flows round and round inside its **blood vessels**. But if your skin gets cut or broken, then blood oozes out of the wound.

A fast seal

Blood defends you by **clotting** – turning into a sticky lump at the wound. It seals the damage to stop itself leaking out, and prevent germs and dirt getting in. Usually clotting enough to stop the bleeding takes only a few minutes. You can help by cleaning the cut as soon as possible, then put on a sticking plaster or maybe a dressing and bandage. This gives added defence against dirt and germs, and also prevents the clot being knocked off.

Medical help

A big wound may leak so fast that the blood cannot clot. So the doctor or nurse puts in stitches (above) or clips. These hold the gap closed so blood can do its defence work.

▼ Under the microscope, a clot is a tangle of tiny fibres, sticky substances and millions of blood cells.

clot   lump of blood that seals a wound
blood vessels   arteries, capillaries, and veins through which blood flows

Clump and clot

Clotting involves about a dozen natural chemicals in blood. It starts with **microscopic** parts in the blood called **platelets**. These are not exactly types of blood cells, but more like pieces of cells. At the damaged area they release substances which make the blood thicker and sticky, and also cause tiny threads to form in the blood. The threads make a tangle that traps blood cells. Gradually the tangle spreads and gets thicker. Over a day or two the clot hardens into a scab which protects the skin beneath while it heals. It then falls off.

HAEMOPHILIA

In the condition called haemophilia, which is inherited (passed on in families), blood lacks certain clotting chemicals. Without these, blood keeps leaking from a wound. Haemophilia can be treated by injections of the missing chemicals.

Plant 'blood'

Plants like pine trees have a defensive fluid called resin. When the tree suffers a cut, sticky resin leaks out and gradually goes hard or 'clots'. Over millions of years lumps of resin become hard yellow amber. Sometimes this contains insects that got trapped in it when it was soft and sticky.

Under invasion!

There are dangers all around you – but they are far too small to see. Germs drift through the air, float in water, and land on objects and surfaces, even when these all look clean. Everything has germs on it – including your body. The body must constantly defend itself against them.

Types of germs

What are the main germs? One group is **bacteria**. The cells of your body are very tiny. Bacteria are even more **microscopic**. About 100,000 would fit into this 'o'. Different bacteria cause problems like sore throats and skin boils as well as serious illnesses like TB (tuberculosis).

Another group of germs is the **viruses**. These are many times smaller even than bacteria.

The good, the bad...

Not all bacteria are harmful germs. Many are harmless, living in the soil. Some are even "friendly" and live inside our own bodies, helping us to take in nourishment from food. Bacteria in yoghurt-type health drinks help our bodies to digest food.

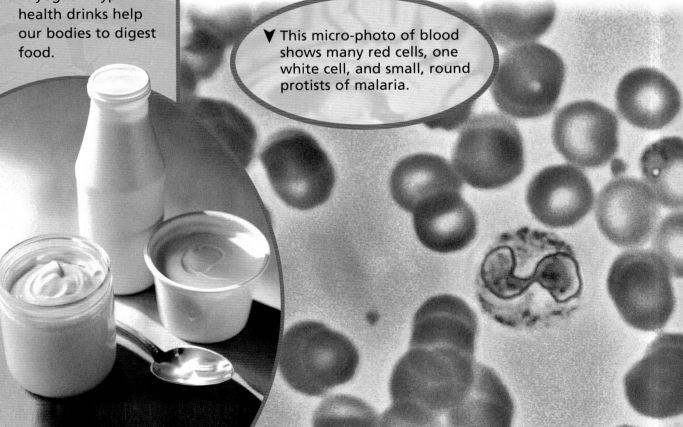

▼ This micro-photo of blood shows many red cells, one white cell, and small, round protists of malaria.

bacteria   microscopic organisms of many types
protists   one-cell organisms, some types causing disease.

Around one million would pile onto the dot on this "i". Viruses cause illnesses like colds, 'flu (influenza) and measles. A third group of germs are **protists**. These are about as big as the body's own cells, and different kinds cause different diseases, such as malaria.

Getting in

Skin is good at keeping out germs. But they are always trying to get into the body – through skin cuts and wounds, by being breathed into the nose, windpipe and lungs, or swallowed in food or drinks. However the body defends all these entrances, as shown on pages 16-33.

...the ugly

All kinds of viruses are harmful. They multiply by getting inside the body's own cells and destroying them. Most viruses are also very tough. They can survive after being dried out, frozen or even boiled.

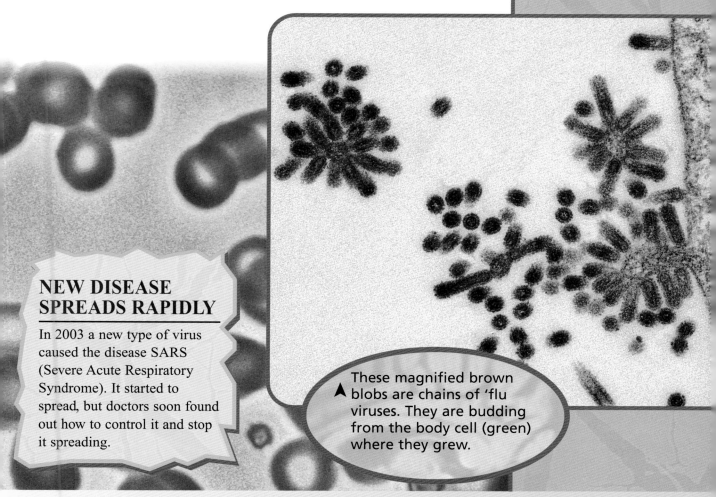

NEW DISEASE SPREADS RAPIDLY

In 2003 a new type of virus caused the disease SARS (Severe Acute Respiratory Syndrome). It started to spread, but doctors soon found out how to control it and stop it spreading.

⋀ These magnified brown blobs are chains of 'flu viruses. They are budding from the body cell (green) where they grew.

The head of a tapeworm is as small as a pin head.

The acid bath

When you eat food and swallow drinks, they go down into your stomach and immediately get attacked. Inside the stomach are very powerful juices, called **enzymes**, and natural acid. Their main task is to **digest** lumps of food into smaller and smaller pieces, to pass into the body.

Chemical defence

The **digestive juices** and acid have an extra use. They help to kill germs which come in with the foods and drinks. The acid attacks each germ's outer covering. This makes the germ unable to multiply, and it can even kill it. This is one of the body's methods of chemical defence.

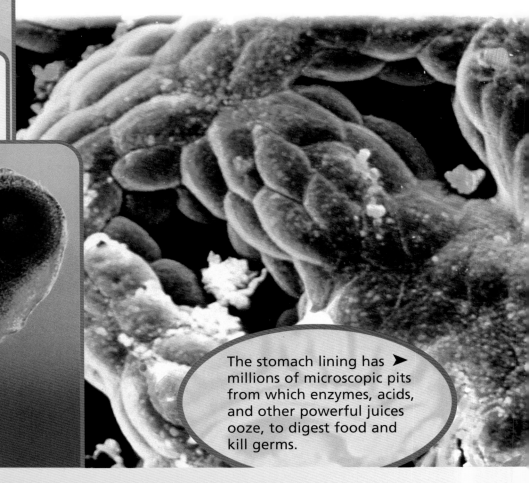

The stomach lining has ➤ millions of microscopic pits from which enzymes, acids, and other powerful juices ooze, to digest food and kill germs.

digest   break down something like food into smaller and smaller pieces
digestive juices   liquids in the digestive system that break food apart

Too many to kill

The stomach's acid and juices can cope with most types of everyday germs. But sometimes unusual germs get in, perhaps in great numbers – many millions. This can happen if we drink unclean water, or eat old, bad food, or food which has not been cooked properly. In these cases, enough germs survive in the stomach to multiply. They then cause types of illness known as food poisoning. Germs which do this include salmonella and listeria.

Help your stomach!

You can help your stomach to defend you in various ways. Avoid foods that look mouldy or bad, or that smell strange or "off". Check use-by or best-before dates. Wash hands well before preparing, cooking and eating food, especially if using your fingers!

Ready and waiting

Special rooms in hospitals and some factories have incredibly clean air, filtered to remove all dust and germs. But for most people, every time we breathe, germs from our environment float into the nose, down the throat and windpipe, and into the lungs. The airway's defences are ready and waiting.

Sticky trap

The insides of the nose, the windpipe, and the lung air tubes are designed to trap dust and germs. Their inner linings continually make the slimy substance **mucus**. Dust and germs get stuck in this mucus and cannot escape. The linings also have millions of micro-hairs called **cilia**. These wave like tiny oars to make the mucus move. It flows like a very slow, sticky river, up the air tubes and windpipe and into the throat. We cough it up and swallow it as **phlegm** when we "clear our throat" – ahem!

When nose is best

The nose has small hairs at its entrance to catch floating dust. And it has its own type of sticky mucus, "snot", to trap germs and other tiny particles. This double defence cleans the air before it gets to the lungs.

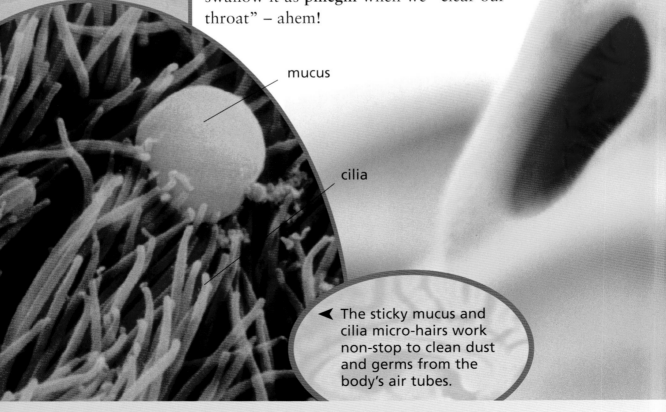

mucus

cilia

◄ The sticky mucus and cilia micro-hairs work non-stop to clean dust and germs from the body's air tubes.

cancer   disease where body cells multiply out of control and may spread, causing growths or lumps called malignant tumours

Not just germs

The airway defence system not only protects against germs. It also traps tiny floating bits of smoke and particles, like those in the exhaust fumes of cars and trucks. If these tiny bits collected in the lungs, they could cause very serious diseases such as **cancer**.

COUGH, SNEEZE

Sometimes a sticky blob of mucus or too much dust gets trapped in the nose. We sneeze to blast air through the nose and blow out the blockage. If the same happens in the windpipe or lower airways, a cough does the same job.

Extra defence

When there are many small particles or droplets floating in air, the body's breathing system may need more protection. A face mask helps to filter out the problem particles. This is very important when working with powders, sprayers, grinders and sanders.

---

cilia   microscopic "hairs" on the cells in various body parts

Battle in the body

When did you last have an infection? What exactly is an "infection"? Every day, some germs manage to get through your body's outer defences, through a tiny cut in your skin, or when you breathe or swallow.

Once inside, the germs have warmth, moisture and nourishment – especially if they are in the blood. So they try to multiply, and spread around the body. An illness caused by germs is known as an infectious disease or infection. If the germs are spread by very close contact (mainly touch), the infection is said to be **contagious**.

In-between time

The 'in-between time' while germs multiply, from catching them to feeling ill, is called the **incubation period**. It varies from a day or two for some germs, to months with others. The person may still be able to pass on the germs to others during the incubation period.

Chickenpox has an incubation period of 12-21 days, then causes itchy spots.

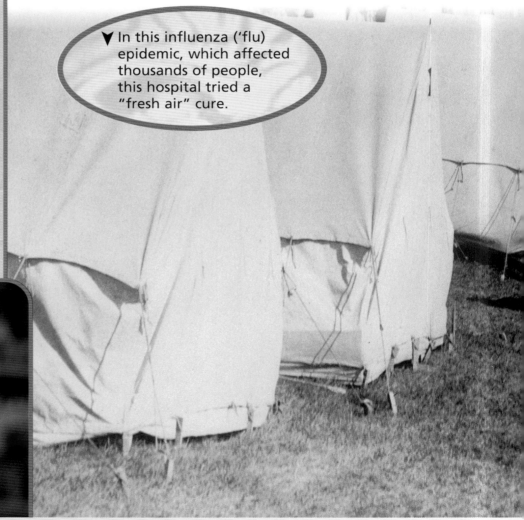

▼ In this influenza ('flu) epidemic, which affected thousands of people, this hospital tried a "fresh air" cure.

contagious   disease caused by germs that is spread by close contact
lymph   pale fluid that flows through vessels and ducts, and joins the blood near the heart

Inner defences

If germs get into the body every day, why aren't we always ill? Because the body not only has outer defences, it has a whole range of inner defences. They involve many body parts, especially the blood, and another body fluid called **lymph**, as well as parts called **lymph nodes** or "glands". All of these are explained on pages 22-33.

Stopping the spread

People with dangerous infections such as ebola (above) may be cared for on their own in hospital isolation rooms. This stops the germs from spreading to other patients. The medical staff wear masks, caps and gowns to keep out the germs.

lymph nodes   parts where white blood cells collect to fight germs, and which become sore during illness

First response

When germs invade or damage occurs, the body starts a process called **inflammation**. White blood cells gather and fluid collects, so that the main defences can begin. This makes the part reddened, swollen, tender and hot at first, but usually the imflammation fades as the defences win.

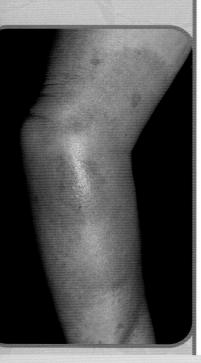

Micro-defenders

Some of your body's best defenders are blobs of pale jelly so small that 1,000 could fit into this "o". Millions of them patrol day and night, on the lookout for germs and other unwanted substances. These champion defenders are called **white blood cells**.

Not well named

The name "white blood cells" is not quite true. They are not white, they are very pale and almost see-through. And not all of them live in the blood. Like tiny plastic bags full of clear jelly, they can change shape to squeeze out of the blood vessels. Then they squash between other body cells, hunting for germs. Since there are blood vessels all over the body, white blood cells can reach every body part.

White blood cells can push  out long, finger-like parts to move and to search for and gather food.

macrophage

macrophage   white blood cell which "eats" bacteria and other unwanted bits

Big eaters

There are several kinds of white blood cells involved in body defences. One kind is the **macrophage** (below). This name simply means "big eater". A macrophage oozes along, searching for germs. When it finds one, it simply flows around it and engulfs it, taking it inside. Within the macrophage, powerful **enzymes** eat into the germ and destroy it.

E.coli bacteria

More defenders

When germs infect the body and multiply, white blood cells mutliply too, as part of the defence system. Their numbers can go up 10 times in two days. This makes the body able to resist the invaders.

AMAZING FACTS

In one drop of blood the size of a pin-head, there are about 5,000 white blood cells.

In the whole body there are 25 million million white blood cells.

Some kinds of white blood cells, like macrophages, live just a few hours and eat more than 100 germs each.

Other kinds of white blood cells survive for many months.

white blood cells   pale cells in the blood which clean blood and fight germs and disease

Coming and going

Lymph does not flow round and round like blood. It starts as watery liquid from inside and around cells, which oozes into the tiny open ends of lymph vessels. The vessels join into larger **ducts**. The two biggest ducts join to blood vessels in the chest, where lymph merges with blood.

Defence highways

Most cities do not rely on one transport system. They have roads, railways, perhaps an underground subway, and maybe even waterways. The body has different transport systems too. These allow its **white blood cells** and other defences to move about quickly, and get straight to the site of trouble. The main two transport systems are blood and **lymph**.

Blood

Blood flows round and round the body in a branching network of **blood vessels,** pumped by the heart. During an infection, white blood cells in the blood search and destroy germs there. The white cells can also move out of the tiniest blood vessels, which are called **capillaries,** to fight any germs among other body cells.

Sometimes a pale ➤ fluid oozes from a graze. This fluid is lymph, and it works with blood to kill germs in the wound.

Body language   ducts   pipes or tubes for liquid
parasitic   when one living thing lives off another, causing damage

Lymph

Sometimes when you have a small cut or graze, no blood comes out. This means you have not damaged a blood vessel. But instead there may be clear or pale fluid, called lymph. Like blood, this flows through the body carrying millions of white blood cells. But it moves much more slowly, because it has no pump of its own. It is pressed and squeezed through its tubes, called lymph vessels, by the muscles around them as the body moves about.

Too much lymph

Rarely, tiny **parasitic** filarial worms get into the lymph system and block its flow. Lymph fluid collects and causes huge swellings. The result is filarial disease, also called "elephantiasis".

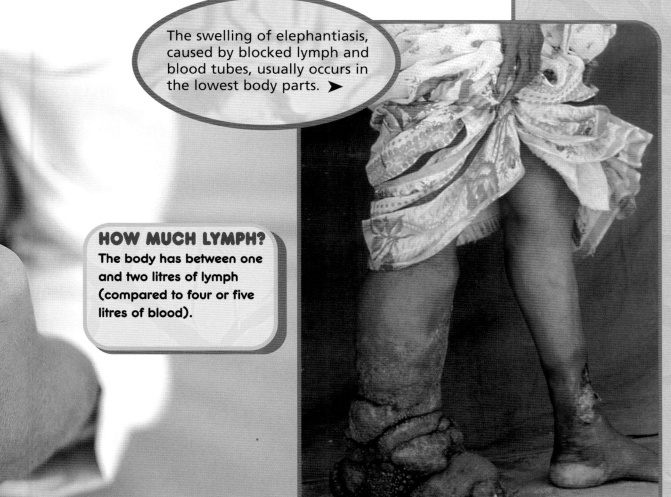

The swelling of elephantiasis, caused by blocked lymph and blood tubes, usually occurs in the lowest body parts. ➤

HOW MUCH LYMPH?
The body has between one and two litres of lymph (compared to four or five litres of blood).

Centres for defence

When people are ill, their "glands" may swell and ache. They form painful lumps under the skin, often in the neck or armpits. These "glands" are called **lymph nodes**, and they are part of the lymph system. There are also lymph nodes in the chest, the lower body or abdomen, and the groin. They also swell during illness, but we cannot feel them as they are deeper within the body. The smallest lymph nodes are the size of rice grains, while larger ones are as big as grapes. But in a serious illness, they can swell as big as tennis balls!

Lymph system

The whole lymph system consists of lymph fluid, lymph vessels and larger tubes called ducts, and lymph nodes.

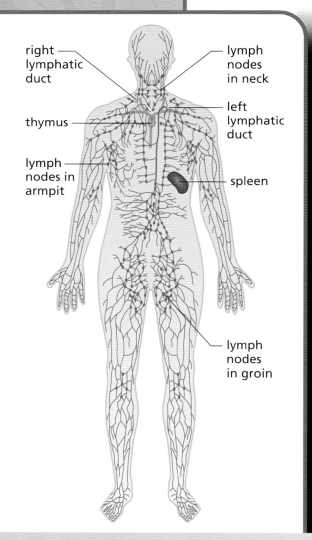

right lymphatic duct

lymph nodes in neck

thymus

left lymphatic duct

lymph nodes in armpit

spleen

lymph nodes in groin

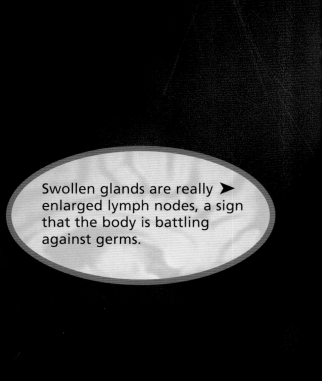

Swollen glands are really ➤ enlarged lymph nodes, a sign that the body is battling against germs.

Packed with defenders

The lymph system's main job is to defend the body by resisting infections and other illnesses. Lymph nodes are centres for this defence. They are packed with white blood cells of many kinds. Some of these multiply rapidly to make more white blood cells. The white cells travel through the lymph and blood systems, and out between the body cells, to combat germs and disease.

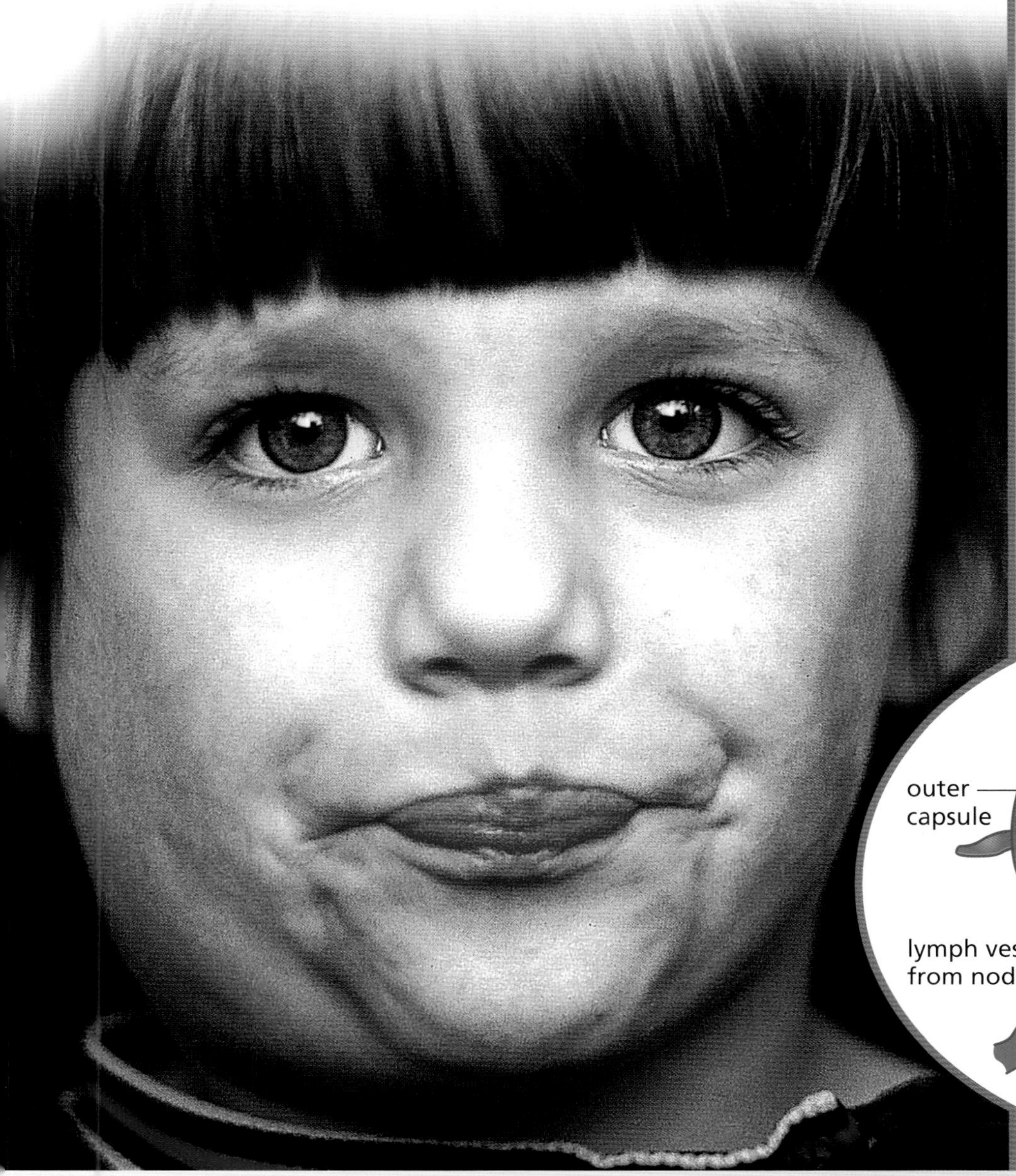

Inside a defence centre

Lymph fluid flows into a node along several tubes, but out along only one. Inside the lymph node, white blood cells multiply to make more of themselves, which then spread around the body to attack germs.

White blood cells multiply in the lymph node's germinal centres.

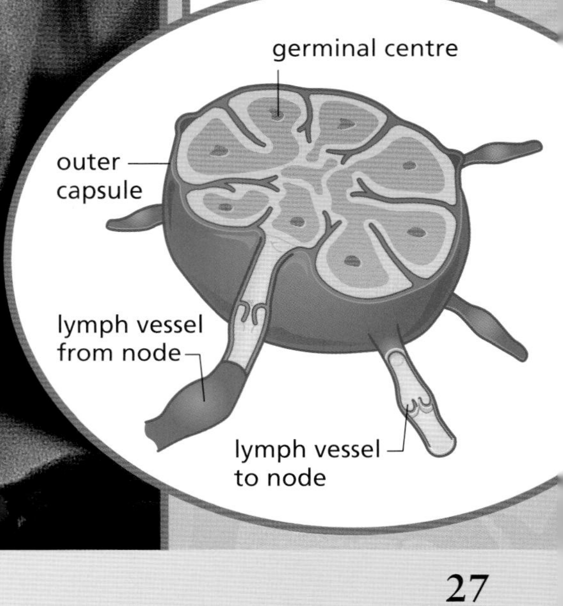

germinal centre

outer capsule

lymph vessel from node

lymph vessel to node

Guarding the entrance

Most parts of the **lymph** defence system are hidden inside the body. But two sets are much nearer the outside. These are the **tonsils** and the **adenoids**. The tonsils are lumpy parts in the throat. They are similar inside to lymph nodes, with many kinds of **white blood cells**. The reason for their position is because they are helping to guard one of the main ways that germs get into the body – through the mouth. The tonsils are well placed to defend against germs in foods and drinks.

Helping to clean air

There are similar lumpy patches called adenoids inside the nose. They also resemble **lymph nodes** inside. They too are well placed to guard a main entrance for germs – the nose. The adenoids help to defend against germs in breathed-in air, and to kill germs trapped by **mucus** (snot) in the nose.

Body gatekeepers

The tonsils are on either side of the upper throat, on the lower edges of the tongue's base. The adenoids are at the lower back of the nasal chamber (the space inside the nose).

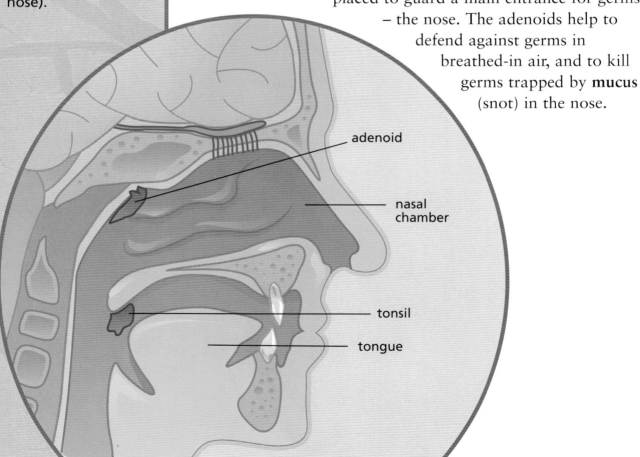

adenoid

nasal chamber

tonsil

tongue

adenoidectomy operation to remove problem adenoids
tonsillectomy operation to remove problem tonsils

Too big

In some younger people, tonsils or adenoids become overactive or "too busy". It is not clear exactly why, but they swell for much of the time. Enlarged tonsils cause a sore throat and painful swallowing. Enlarged adenoids make the voice sound odd, and block the nose so the person breathes through the mouth.

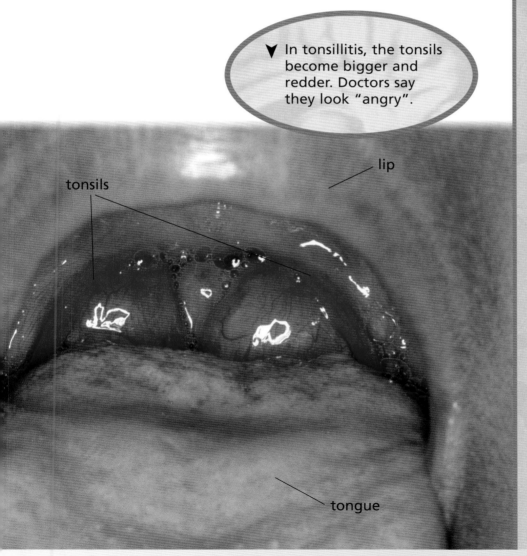

▼ In tonsillitis, the tonsils become bigger and redder. Doctors say they look "angry".

tonsils

lip

tongue

Treatment

Sometimes swollen tonsils and adenoids are part of a general illness. But if they stay too big for too long, they can be removed by an operation. This is **tonsillectomy** or **adenoidectomy**.

"I had swollen tonsils for years. Normally doctors don't take them out. After they did, I could swallow properly again."

Allan, aged 14.

Your ever-ready army

Training camp

The **thymus** is a body part just behind the breastbone, shaped like two sausages side by side. It is part of the **lymph** system, as the main "training site" for the white blood cells called lymphocytes. This is where the lymphocytes multiply and gain their germ-fighting powers. "Trained" lymphocytes are called **T-cells** (T for thymus).

Have you ever visited an old castle, with its water-filled moat, massive walls and tall inner towers? Well-defended places like castles and fortresses have many lines of defence. Your body is the same. If germs get past the outer defences, and even the first inner defences, then the body has an army inside to fight them.

The defence deep inside is the **immune system**. It involves various groups of **white blood cells** and other cells, as well as various natural chemicals. All these move around the body in the blood and lymph, to wherever they are needed. The immune system also acts against illnesses which are not caused by germs from outside, but which start inside the body, like some forms of **cancer**.

donor person who gives something
immune system cells and body parts which protect the body from illness

Chief defenders

The main defenders in the immune system are the white blood cells called **lymphocytes**. Like other white blood cells they can change shape and move anywhere to reach every part. Millions die each day in the battle against germs and disease. So the body makes millions more. They are produced in the jelly-like marrow inside bones. The **bone marrow** makes other kinds of white blood cells too, as well as **red blood cells** which carry oxygen around the body.

▼ If you don't manage to get out of the way of someone sneezing, the germs will find their way inside you – so you need your immune system.

Bone marrow transplant

In some people the immune system's lymphocytes do not work properly. One treatment is bone marrow **transplant**. Marrow from another person, the **donor**, is injected into the bones. This healthy marrow should then make fully working lymphocytes.

DESPERATELY SEEKING A DONOR!

In a bone marrow transplant (right), the bone marrow must be specially selected as exactly the right type or "match" for the patient. Otherwise the patient's immune system will try to fight against it, and lose even more strength.

lymphocytes types of white blood cells that fight germs
thymus body part near the heart that is part of the lymph system

The protection squad

How would you recognize your friends in a crowd? It would be easy if they all wore tall, bright yellow hats. A similar problem occurs in the body. How do white blood cells like **lymphocytes** recognize germs, especially if they have no tall hats? And once recognized, how do lymphocytes destroy them and tell the germs apart from the body cells?

Telling apart

All kinds of germs have an outer layer or "skin". They carry special marker substances called **antigens**, which identify them. So do the body's cells. But the antigens on germs are different. Certain types of lymphocytes, the **T-cells**, can recognize these different substances, and tell the germs from the cells.

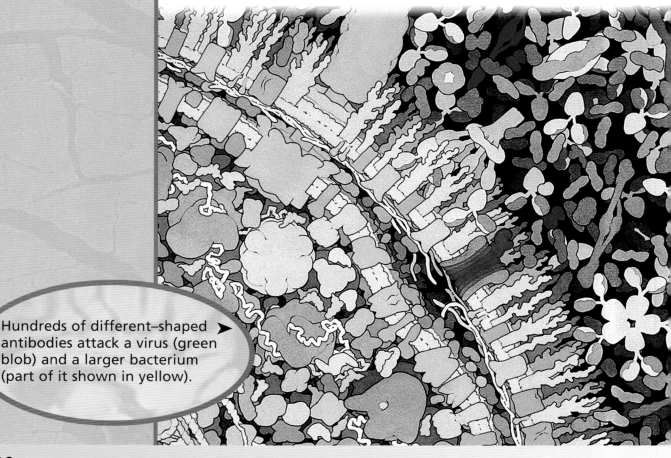

Hundreds of different–shaped ▶ antibodies attack a virus (green blob) and a larger bacterium (part of it shown in yellow).

Not only that, the lymphocytes can recognize the exact type of germ. These lymphocytes then instruct other types of lymphocytes, called **B-cells**, to make one of the immune system's main weapons – **antibodies**.

Germ warfare

Antibodies are body chemicals designed to fight germs. They float in the blood and **lymph**. Each kind of antibody is specially shaped to fit onto the antigen of a particular type of germ. When the antibody locks on, it makes the germ fall apart, or stops it multiplying. During an infection, this happens every second to thousands or millions of germs all over the body. Gradually the germs die or are destroyed.

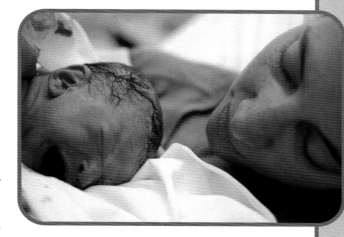

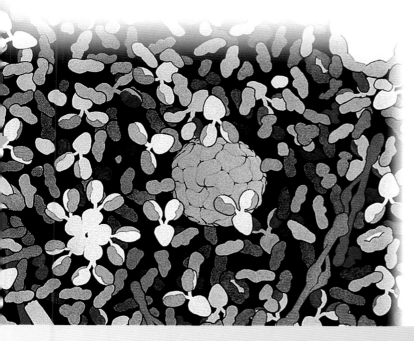

Ready-made 1

A new baby takes in antibodies from its mother, both in the womb, and after it's born, when it drinks her milk. These ready-made antibodies protect the baby against certain diseases for a time, until its own immune system develops and becomes stronger.

Ready-made 2

People travelling to places where certain diseases are common may have an injection. This contains ready-made antibodies against the germs for those diseases. This is not the same as the body making its own antibodies, as explained on pages 34-35.

antigens substances which are not part of the body, and are recognized and attacked by the immune system (with antibodies)

Tricking the defences

Can you remember having some injections when you were young? You may have had one recently too. These injections protect you against certain serious, even deadly diseases. What is in these injections and how do they work?

Long memories

After a germ infects you, some of your **lymphocytes** become "memory cells". They remember how to make the **antibodies** that fight the germ. If the same germs get into your body later, the immune system can make massive amounts of the correct antibody quickly. The germs are destroyed before they can multiply and cause disease. This is known as becoming **resistant** or **immune** to that infection.

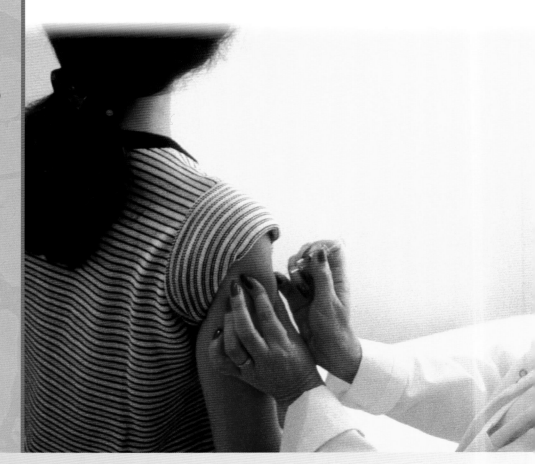

toxin   harmful or poisonous chemical or substance

Fooling the system

To protect you against germs that you might come across in the future, your immune system can be "tricked" into making the special antibodies that you will need. You have probably had a **vaccination** before. The **vaccine** contains dead or disabled versions of the germs. Or it may contain harmless versions of the **toxins** made by the germs. Your immune system thinks it is under attack and responds as usual by making antibodies.

First time round, building defences to new germs like this takes time. If you had "caught" the germs in the normal way, they would multiply and make you ill. But the 'fake' germs in the vaccine cannot cause the proper illness, so there is no disease. This makes it easy for your immune system to build up its weapons.

The immune system is now ready to combat the germs much more quickly the next time, if you caught the germs later in life. The whole process of becoming resistant is called **immunization**.

Changing germs

Vaccines do not work against some diseases, like the common cold. The virus germs which cause this are always changing their **antigens**. The body becomes resistant to one version, but does not recognize the next, and so on. So we cannot be immune, and get colds most years.

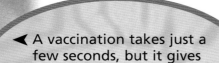

◀ A vaccination takes just a few seconds, but it gives many years of protection from a serious disease.

---

vaccine   substance containing harmless versions of a germ, which makes the immune system able to defend against the real germs

Asthma

In some people **asthma** attacks can be triggered by a tiny creature, the dust mite (below). It lives in house dust, and like all animals, produces droppings. These dry out and float as powder. In the lungs, an allergic reaction to the droppings makes the airways tighten up, making breathing wheezy and difficult.

Harmless yet harmful

Do you know someone who gets **asthma** or **hay fever**? Maybe you get them yourself. These conditions are called **allergies**. They are caused by the system which is supposed to protect the body – the **immune system**. They happen when the system goes wrong for some reason, although it is not clear why.

Mistaken identity

The immune system is supposed to defend the body against germs and harmful substances. An allergy is a case of mistaken identity.

If you are allergic, your immune system attacks substances that do not bother other people at all. In hay fever, the harmless substance is the tiny **pollen** grains of plants like grasses, trees and flowers.

allergic reaction processes such as inflammation or coughing as the body fights a substance that is harmless to most people

These float in the air like specks of dust too small to see, mainly in spring and summer, and we all breathe them in.

Over–reacting!

Inside the nose of a person with hay fever, the immune system goes into action as if the pollen grains were germs. The nose swells inside and becomes runny, itchy and sneezy. The same may happen when pollen touches the eyes, making the eyes runny, red and itchy. This is your immune system overreacting and trying to get rid of the pollen.

◄ Pollen from grasses and crops like wheat is spread by the wind, and also by machines like combine harvesters!

Treatments

There are several kinds of inhalers or "puffers" for allergic conditions like hay fever and asthma. They deliver medical drugs direct to the site of the problem – up the nose in hay fever, and deep into the lungs for asthma.

FOOD ALLERGIES

Certain foods cause allergic reactions in some people, including peanuts, shellfish and strawberries.

The reaction can make the face swell and the skin go red with a rash. The airways can even close up and this can kill.

People with severe food allergies should carry medicines all the time in case they accidentally eat one of the danger foods.

asthma condition, often linked to allergy, where the bronchioles get narrow and fill with mucus, making breathing difficult

No immunity

Some babies are born with an immune system that does not work. The cause is often unknown. With no defence against germs, the baby must stay in special germ-free surroundings (like the one below). One hope of treatment is a **bone marrow transplant.**

Defences down

One of the newest and most serious diseases around the world is **AIDS**. It is a problem of the immune system. This becomes deficient, which means it cannot work properly. AIDS is caused by a virus known as **HIV**. This can be spread by sexual contact with someone who has HIV, or by using drug equipment such as needles and syringes already used by someone with HIV/AIDS. It can also be passed from a mother with HIV to her baby.

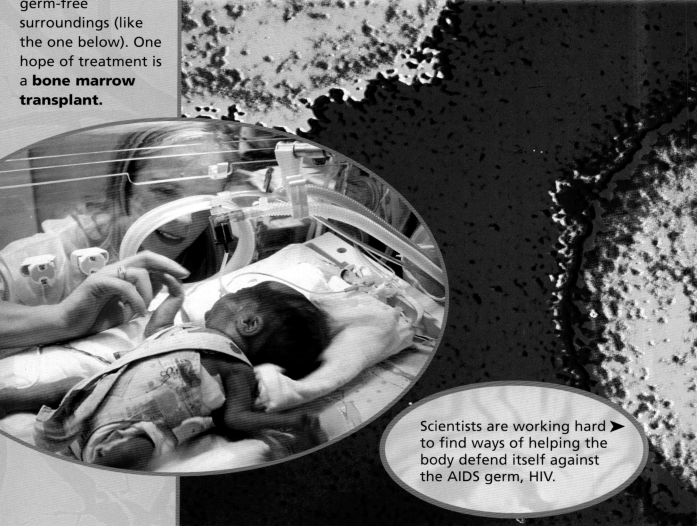

Scientists are working hard ➤ to find ways of helping the body defend itself against the AIDS germ, HIV.

AIDS Aquired Immune Deficiency Syndrome, caused by HIV
HIV Human Immunodeficiency Virus which affects the immune system and causes AIDS

Attacking the defenders

HIV attacks the body's defences. In particular it targets the types of **lymphocytes** called T4 cells, which are an essential part of the immune system. Without them, the immune defences break down. Germs can multiply more easily. People with AIDS begin to suffer from infections such as tuberculosis and pneumonia. Medical drugs can slow down the development of AIDS greatly. At present there is no **vaccine** to prevent infection, and no cure.

Damping down

It may be useful to "calm down" the body's immune system so it works less well, using **immuno–suppressive** drugs. This happens when someone receives a transplant such as a heart, liver or kidney. Otherwise the body would defend itself by rejecting this strange new object inside it.

SELF-ATTACK

In some people the immune system defends not against germs, or even harmless items like pollen, but against the body itself. Such problems are called **auto-immune disorders**. They include certain forms of diabetes, psoriasis, and multiple sclerosis.

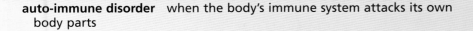

auto-immune disorder   when the body's immune system attacks its own body parts

Stay out of danger!

No worries!

Every day we do dozens of things that hardly seem dangerous at all, like crossing the road (like the couple below), or even chewing our food. We've done it so many times, we don't pay attention. But these familiar actions are often when people get hurt or even killed. Defending yourself needs constant care and awareness.

Your body has an amazing set of defences, from your outer skin, to sticky linings in your airways, acid in your stomach, blood that clots, and the germ-killing **immune system** deep inside. But there are many other ways you can defend yourself, simply by thinking. You can make choices. By thinking about what you do beforehand, you can defend yourself in advance. In this way you can take better care of your body.

Safer danger

You probably get tempted to do dares or take small risks sometimes. In fact nearly everything we do carries some risk. Avoiding all danger is boring. Risks can be exciting, give us a buzz, and make life interesting. However, there are ways of making risks safer.

Whether it is playing sport, making new friends, visiting an unknown place, learning a new skill like rock-climbing or skydiving – we can plan ahead, to reduce the dangers. For example, we can read maps or wear the right clothing when we go exploring. By taking responsibility for your own body in this way you protect yourself, prevent harm, and stay happier and healthier.

Amazing stunts like these ▼ don't come easily. They need plenty of practice, and perhaps coaching from an expert – but the results are well worth it.

BIG SHOCK PUTS MAN IN HOSPITAL

A local man was rushed to Sydney hospital yesterday suffering from electric shock. He was cleaning the glass in his fish tank with a scraper blade, when he accidentally sliced through the cable to the water heater. Medical staff said he was very lucky to be alive.

Many serious accidents happen in familiar situations when people forget to take proper care.

Medical help

Doctors and medicines can assist the body's defences in many ways. **Antibiotic** drugs work against **bacterial** germs that cause infection. Killing viruses is much more difficult. Scientists are only now beginning to develop **antiviral** drugs that work.

Resist and defend

Your body can only defend itself well if it is strong. Otherwise its defence systems cannot work, making infections and other illnesses more likely. Apart from babies and young children, the responsibility for a healthy, fit body lies mainly with its owner. You need to be aware of what keeps you healthy and what is harmful, and make the best choices you can.

Not so obvious

Sometimes the effects of our choices are not so obvious. Staying up very late often, or skipping meals, may seem harmless. But it makes the body run down and tired, and lacking energy. Gradually its levels of stress go up. The body's defences are so busy with these, they are less able to resist germs and illness.

Keep fighting fit if you ➤ want your immune system to defend you.

antibiotic   substance that acts against bacteria
antiviral   substance that acts against viruses

Also the defences work better if the body has a varied diet, with lots of fresh fruits and vegetables, and not too much salt or fatty animal foods. For example, a poor diet can make the skin thinner and more brittle. Then it is more likely to split open when injured and let in germs.

Self defence

Your body defences might seem complicated and separate from the outside world. They involve chemical substances and billions of **microscopic** cells deep within us. But the risks and dangers you need protection from are affected by what you do, think, say, eat and choose – that's all up to you.

Destroying defences

Everyone knows that smoking tobacco does great damage to the body. One of its effects is to kill the tiny **cilia** hairs that sweep dust and germs out of the lungs. Yet still people smoke. Is each cigarette really worth all the harm it does?

Find out more

Places to visit

The Natural History Museum in London has a human biology gallery. There, you can hear what a baby hears in the womb, see how bones and muscles work together, and find out all about the amazing human body.

Natural History Museum, Cromwell Road, London, SW7 5BD

www.nhm.ac.uk

Books

The Immune System: Injury, Illness and Health, Carol Ballard (Heinemann Library, 2003)

Pox, Pus and Plague: a history of disease and infection, John Townsend (Raintree, 2005)

Body: An Amazing Tour of Human Anatomy, Robert Winston (Dorling Kindersley, 2005)

World Wide Web

If you want to find out more about the immune system, you can search the Internet using keywords like these:

- 'immune system'
- asthma + dust
- hay fever

You can also find your own keywords by using headings or words from this book.

Search tips

There are billions of pages on the Internet so it can be difficult to find exactly what you are looking for. These search tips will help you find useful websites quickly:

- Use simple keywords instead of whole sentences
- Use two to six keywords in a search, putting the most important words first
- Be precise – only use names of people, places or things
- If you want to find words that go together, put quote marks around them, for example 'stomach acid' or 'length of intestine'
- Use the advanced section of your search engine
- Use the + sign between keywords to link them, for example typing + KS3 after your keyword will help you find web pages at the right level.

Where to search

Search engine
A search engine looks through the entire web and lists all sites that match the words in the search box. It can give thousands of links, but the best matches are at the top of the list, on the first page. Try **bbc.co.uk/search**

Search directory
A search directory is like a library of websites that have been sorted by a person instead of a computer. You can search by keyword or subject and browse through the different sites like you look through books on a library shelf. A good example is **yahooligans.com**

Glossary

adenoidectomy operation to remove problem adenoids

adenoids patches in the nasal chamber which are part of the lymph system

AIDS Aquired Immune Deficiency Syndrome, caused by HIV

allergic reaction processes such as inflammation or coughing as the body fights a substance that is harmless to most people

allergy when the body reacts to a substance that is normally harmless, like pollen

antibiotic substance that acts against bacteria

antibodies substances made by the immune system which attack antigens

antigens substances which are not part of the body, and are recognized and attacked by the immune system (with antibodies)

antiviral substance that acts against viruses

asthma condition, often linked to allergy, where the bronchioles get narrow and fill with mucus, making breathing difficult

auto-immune disorder when the body's immune system attacks its own body parts

bacteria microscopic organisms of many types

B-cell type of white blood cell that makes antibodies to attack germs

blood vessels arteries, capillaries, and veins through which blood flows

calluses patches of thick, hardened skin

cancer disease where body cells multiply out of control and may spread, causing growths or lumps called malignant tumours

capillaries tiniest blood vessels with very thin walls

cells microscopic "building blocks" that make up all body parts

cilia microscopic "hairs" on the cells in various body parts

clot lump of blood that seals a wound

contagious disease caused by germs that is spread by close contact

dermis inner layer of skin containing sweat glands, hair roots and nerve sensors

digest break down something like food into smaller and smaller pieces

digestive juices liquids in the digestive system that break food apart

donor person who gives something

ducts pipes or tubes for liquid

enzyme substance that controls the speed of a chemical change

epidermis outer layer of skin, constantly renewed from underneath

HIV Human Immunodeficiency Virus which affects the immune system and causes AIDS

immune system cells and body parts which protect the body from illness

immune resistant to a certain infection and able to destroy the germs before they multiply and cause illness

immunization the process of becoming resistant, or immune, to a certain illness

immuno-suppressive "damps down" the body's immune system to make it less sensitive

incubation period the time between germs getting into the body and when the effects or symptoms of illness begin

inflammation body's response to damage, germs or disease, where fluids collect and white cells gather to fight germs, causing redness, swelling, pain, and heat

keratin tough, protein-type substance that makes skin resistant to wear

lymph nodes body parts where white blood cells collect to fight germs, and which become swollen during illness

lymph pale fluid that flows through vessels and ducts and joins the blood near the heart

lymphocytes types of white blood cells that fight germs

macrophage white blood cell which "eats" bacteria and other unwanted bits

microscopic something so small that it can only be seen under a microscope

mucus sticky fluid in various body parts, to gather bits of dust and germs, and help substances slip past easily

parasitic when one living thing lives off another, causing damage

phlegm sticky fluid from the airways, especially coughed up from the lungs

platelets bits of cells that take part in clotting

pollen tiny dust-like particles or grains released by plant flowers as part of their breeding process to make seeds

protists one-cell organisms, some types causing disease

red blood cells cells specialized to carry oxygen around the body

reflexes automatic reactions like blinking or coughing

resistant protected against or able to resist an illness

sebum oily substance made by skin to protect itself and stay flexible

thymus body part near the heart that is part of the lymph system

tonsillectomy operation to remove problem tonsils

tonsils patches inside the throat which are part of the lymph system

toxin harmful or poisonous chemical or substance

transplant when a body substance or part is replaced by another in the same body, or from one body to another

vaccination putting a vaccine into the body to make it immune to a certain disease

vaccine substance containing harmless versions of a germ, which makes the immune system able to defend against the real germs

viruses tiniest germs, which can cause serious diseases

white blood cells pale cells in the blood which clean blood and fight germs and disease

Index